RESPECT!

AT HOME

Kate Brookes

HODDER
Wayland

an imprint of Hodder Children's Books

Other titles in the series
At School
Growing Up
In the Street

For more information on this series and other Hodder Wayland titles, go to www.hodderwayland.co.uk

Editor: Sarah Doughty
Photostylist: Gina Brown
Specially commissioned photographs: Pat Aithie and Angela Hampton. With thanks to Grace Jackaman for her assistance in providing models.
Designer: Simon Borrough
Illustrator: Mike Flanagan

First published in 1999 by Wayland Publishers Ltd

This paperback edition published in 2005 by Hodder Wayland, an imprint of Hodder Children's Books

British Library Cataloguing in Publication Data
Brookes, Kate
    At Home. – (Young Citizen)
    1. Citizenship – Juvenile Literature
    2. Ethics – Juvenile literature
    I. Title
    172.1

ISBN 0 7502 4776 2

Printed in China by WKT Company Limited

Hodder Children's Books
A division of Hodder Headline Limited
338 Euston Road, London NW1 3BH

CONTENTS

ALL FAMILIES ARE DIFFERENT

Even though you and your best friend may live in similar homes in the same neighbourhood and may have the same number of parents, brothers and sisters, guinea pigs and goldfish, your families are very different. And because families are different, home life is different.

Every family is unique – there's no family exactly like another. This makes every family – including yours – very special.

ONE OF A KIND?

Janine lives with her Mum

"My Mum looks after me since my Dad no longer lives with us. I look forward to seeing my Dad at weekends and sometimes he is there to pick me up from school when my Mum is at work." **Janine**

Here's Jude and her family

"I have two younger brothers, Joel and Emile. I help Dad with the chores while Mum looks after baby Joel. I feel responsible for helping out with my younger brothers." **Jude**

Shadi and her sister have a foster brother

"My Mum and Dad have fostered a little boy, Mark. We really like playing with him and helping him and he's become an important part of our family." **Shadi**

Sean lives with his sister and grandparents

"Living with Gran and Pa was really awful to start with. They were so strict. I think they worried that something might happen to us. But now we're one happy family!"

Sean

Joshua lives with his Mum, stepfather, sister and new baby brother

"Since getting remarried, Mum has a new baby to think about. My step dad is nice but Jane and I used to have Mum all to ourselves; now we have to share her."

Joshua

Naomi, an only child, lives with her Mum and Dad

"My friends think I'm lucky being an only child. They say brothers and sisters are a pain. I don't know; my parents try and make things fun for me but sometimes I get quite lonely." **Naomi**

Top secret – for your eyes only

Grab a pencil and paper and describe your family. Write down five things that make your family wonderful and five things that really bug you. As you read this book, look out for ways to squash those annoying things that bug you.

When you were a baby, you needed to be cared for by your family. You couldn't leap out of your cot and rustle up a pot of spicy noodles, for instance.

Now you're older you want to take a bit of control of Spaceship My Life. You can raid the fruit bowl if you're hungry, find something to wear, switch on the telly, go play with your mates and keep yourself amused for hours. It may feel like you're growing out of your family.

This feeling gets stronger when you're in strife or have lots of chores to do or if there's trouble in the family. Sometimes it seems as though Spaceship My Life would be a whole heap more fun without your family on board. But would it?

1. "I am in full control of My Life! I can make decisions about where I go, I can look after myself and I know what I like!"

2. "Help! My family are invading My Life! Let me steer a course away from them! Let's try this planet on my own away from my family!"

THE BIG QUESTION

What would life be like on the lonely planet without your family on board?

FAMILY FACTS

1. Families aren't perfect
2. Families are made up of individuals who, just like you, have opinions about everything
3. Families are affected by things that happen outside the home
4. There are ups and downs in every family

WHAT CAN A FAMILY GIVE YOU?
Which of these are the most important?

Love   Laughs

Trust

Protection

Respect

Satellite TV

Security

In-line skates

Warmth

Food

THE BIG QUESTION

What can YOU give back to your family?

7

IT'S NOT FAIR!

RULES, RULES AND MORE RULES

You don't need to be told that there are lots of rules. There are rules that keep you safe and well, and there are family rules that help you to live together peacefully (well, that's the idea).

Hi; I'm Harriet, and this is my brother Jake, and my sister Rosie. We've got some rules in our house. Look and see if we are keeping them!

Lights out time!

We turn lights out by 9 pm on school nights.

Mum, I'm going outside to play.

We can go outside but we must tell our parents that we are leaving the house.

Haven't you fed the fish yet?

We have to remember to look after our pets!

Here are our other rules
Don't cross the road without an adult
Put dirty clothes in the basket for washing
Help clear the table after tea
Don't allow the cat to sleep on our beds
If we make a mess, we have to tidy it up

We mustn't muck around near the stove
Don't leave the top off the toothpaste
Always remember to flush the toilet and then wash your hands
Don't let the soap go all mushy in the bath
No TV till homework and chores are done
No fibbing

YOU BE THE JUDGE

What do you think about these rules? Are they fair or unfair?

Which are rules about keeping safe and which are family rules?

Do these rules help everyone in the family?

Should the parents stick to these rules as well?

Breaking the rules

"There's lots of TV shows that I'm not allowed to watch. When I ask why, my Mum says 'Because I say so'. She's so bossy!"
Shivali

Do you think Shivali will watch banned programmes? Why? If this happened to you, would you break the rule or talk about it with a parent?

RULES FOR A REASON

Rules make more sense when you know there is a reason for them.

"My parents wouldn't let me go to see this dead spooky film. I asked them why and they said it was too violent and gory. I suppose they were right." **David**

MAKING THE RULES

"I'm not allowed to use rude words but my Dad is always swearing. I told him that it wasn't fair that there was one rule for me and another for him. We talked about it and then the family made up a new rule: no one can use rude words. So far no one's broken this rule." **Billy**

What Billy did
1. Realized that something was unfair
2. Talked to his father about it
3. Got his whole family involved
4. Together they made up a new rule that they all agreed to respect.
   Is Billy a budding lawyer or what?!

THE BIG QUESTION

If a person commits a crime and breaks the law, they are punished. Should there be punishments for breaking rules at home?

PRIVATE KEEP OUT!

What's your biggest peeve about privacy? It is that your brother borrows your stuff without asking, your sister uses up your bubble bath and doesn't replace it, or that while you're at school your room is tidied and all your fave things are moved so that you can't find them? It doesn't matter how your privacy is being invaded, it's really annoying isn't it?

Irene and Nuala are twins. They're really close and share lots of things but sometimes the sharing goes too far ...

Both Nuala and Irene want their privacy. Nuala doesn't want Irene borrowing her stuff without asking, and Irene certainly doesn't want her secret thoughts becoming public knowledge.

Here are some suggestions that may solve their problem.

"They could tell their parents but I don't think this will help. Nuala and Irene have to work it out for themselves." **Trish**

"There's no excuse for reading someone's diary. I bet Irene doesn't trust her now. Nuala is going to have to prove she can be trusted." **Scarlet**

"Nuala and Irene should make an agreement about borrowing each other's stuff. Me and my older brother worked out that some things were okay to borrow and some not." **Matt**

"If they can't trust each other then Nuala's going to have to lock her wardrobe and Irene will have to keep her diary with her." **Marie-Anne**

"If they both start respecting each other's privacy, then this won't happen again." **Tom**

THE BIG QUESTION

Which suggestion would you try if you were Nuala or Irene?

Are You a Snoop?

Privacy is not just about protecting your things. It's also about being able to have secret thoughts (such as those in Irene's diary), time by yourself and private conversations. How do you and your family rate when it comes to respecting each other's privacy?

Try this quiz to find out:

1. You're having a serious natter on the phone. Does your family …

a) leave the room but ask later for all the gossip?

b) eavesdrop?

c) mind their own business?

2. You're at a friend's house and the parents have an enormous argument. Do you …

a) listen real hard?

b) soak in every detail so that you can tell everyone?

c) go somewhere so that you can't hear what's going on?

3. You've found where your parents have hidden your birthday present. Do you …

a) feel it to get an idea of what it is but that's all?

b) chuckle that nobody can keep secrets from you and open it?

c) try to forget all about it?

4. A letter arrives for your twin sister with some juicy gossip. Do you ...

a) hold it up to the light in the hope that you can read something?

b) open it, read it and then blab all the juicy bits?

c) do nothing, knowing that it is illegal to open someone else's mail?

HOW DID YOU DO?

Mostly As: You know what privacy means but you're only one step away from being a snoop.

Mostly Bs: B is for bad. You don't seem to care at all for other people's privacy. Watch out for a sticky end.

Mostly Cs: You've got your privacy sussed and you respect your family's right to privacy.

THE BIG QUESTION

It is OK to keep some things secret from your family?

Dear Diary ...
Everyone knows that a diary is very personal, but it's hard to resist the temptation to sneak a peek. What would you do in these situations?

✱ You find an old private diary belonging to your Mum or Dad. Would you read it?

✱ You're worried that someone in your family is in trouble. Is that a good excuse for reading their diary?

✱ Would you keep a diary if you knew that it might be read?

13

BUT HIS DAD SAYS IT'S OK!

All families are different and that's why your parents may not let you do something that your best friend's parents allow. But why are families so different? It's because they have different beliefs, values and traditions.

CAN YOU IDENTIFY WITH ANY OF THESE?

"I'm Jewish and go to synagogue on Saturday. That means I can't play football. I really miss it but following my religion is more important." **Adam**

"I can't play with my friends after school because I help out in my Mum's shop. She says that it helps me to accept responsibility. My Mum worked in the shop when she was my age." **Shaneen**

"I want to have my ears pierced. My best friend had his done ages ago. My Dad says that I have to wait until I'm an adult." **Jo**

While you and your family may agree on some things, you will have your own ideas about lots of other things. This is why you and a parent may disagree about what you wear, where you go and even about what you eat!

So what do they mean?
A **belief** is something you believe. You may follow the beliefs of your religion.
Values are things or ideas that you think are important. If you value the environment, you will do your best to protect it.
A **tradition** is something handed down from earlier generations. A tradition in many families is to have a special meal together.

"I'm the only vegetarian in my family. I've tried to tell them that eating meat is cruel to animals but they don't understand my views!" **Andrew**

Value packed

There are many values that everyone agrees about.
These values help us to live together.

Here are some good values and what they mean.	Meaning
Honesty	Being truthful to yourself and to others.
Respect	Treating everyone politely. Doing nothing to hurt yourself or other things that are important.
Tolerance	Accepting that people should be able to follow their culture and beliefs.
Sharing	Being happy to 'give' to other people.
Loyalty	Being honest and faithful.
Kindness	Being thoughtful and caring.

Are there any other values that you would like to add?

WORDS INTO ACTION
Which values are being put into action in these scenes?

It'll be better if you own up to it.

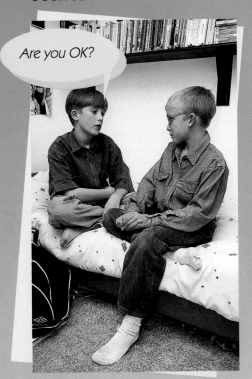

Are you OK?

Thanks for helping me make something vegetarian.

YOU CAN TRUST ME. PROMISE!

Trust is about believing in someone. If a parent says they will pick you up from school or from the swimming pool, you trust them to show up. The parent is also showing their trust in you. They trust you to be waiting for them in a safe place and not walking home alone.

How does your family show that they trust you?

"As long as I wear my helmet and stay in the cycle lane my Grandma lets me cycle to my friend's house and to the shops in town." **Michael**

"I'm diabetic and that means eating properly and doing my blood tests. When I was younger, my Mum did all the checking. Now she trusts me to do it myself."
Giles

BEING TRUSTED – IT'S ALL GOOD NEWS!

As you get older it's more important that you can be trusted. If you can be trusted to go where you say you will go and to be back at an agreed time, then you'll be trusted to go out alone or with your friends.

Here are some other good reasons for being trusted:

You'll be given more independence. **Yes!**

You'll be able to choose your own clothes, TV programmes and music. **Yes!**

Your opinions about life, love and lilac nail varnish will be respected. **Good one!**

You'll like yourself heaps! **Cool.**

Nag sessions about homework will disappear! **Hooray!**

You'll be left alone with a box of chocolates. (Is this pushing the trust thing too far?)

WHEN TRUST GOES WRONG

Hi! What have you been doing?

None of your business, squirt.

I've got enough money to buy that game now.

Oh no! All my money's gone. Amanda's stolen it!

I can't believe she'd do that.

I didn't do it. Why doesn't anybody believe me?

WHAT HAS HAPPENED IN THIS STORY?

Do you think Amanda's family will trust her again?

How can she regain their trust?

What should Amanda have done?

DOUBLE TROUBLE

Look how one breach of trust creates another breach of trust.

"When my Mum said that I could go swimming with my older brother, she made us promise that we would stay together. We were having great fun until John bumped into some mates. They started teasing me and calling me names. John laughed and swam away with his mates. He left me behind. That's when it happened – this big kid did a bomb and landed on top of me. The lifeguard had to jump in to get me. In the First Aid room John made me promise that I wouldn't tell mum. I won't go out with him again because I don't trust him." **Jason**

THE BIG QUESTION

Shouldn't there be complete trust in families?

Family in St.ife

Family problems come in all shapes and sizes. Some blow over quickly, others upset everyone for a long time. But there are some problems that can cause a family to be torn in two.

"My Mum drinks too much. She can't get out of bed in the morning. I try to help her by telling everyone that's she's not well." **Melody**

"My parents divorced last year. In a way, I'm glad — there's no shouting anymore." **Max**

"Dad looks after us, but he works a lot so we hardly see him. I'd love to spend more time with him." **Annabel**

"We've never had enough money for treats and holidays but we were OK. But since Dad lost his job it's been horrible. Dad's always angry and our Mum is sad." **Josh**

"No matter how hard I try in what I do, I get into trouble. I can't do anything to make my family happy. Is there something wrong with me?" **Duncan**

These things can happen in any family. And while not all can have happy endings, there are ways of helping yourself and maybe even your family.

10 things to remember

1. If an adult is in trouble, it's not your fault.

2. Don't try to cope alone, ask for help.

3. Don't tell stories to cover up for an adult in trouble.

4. Talk to someone you trust – an adult is usually best.

5. Everyone can make mistakes.

6. Arguing or ignoring each other won't solve the problem.

7. Don't hide what you're feeling, talk it out.

8. No one has the right to hurt you or to shout horrible things at you.

9. No one can run away from problems.

10. Sorry – a little word that can make all the difference. Everyone should try using it!

SAM WORKS IT OUT

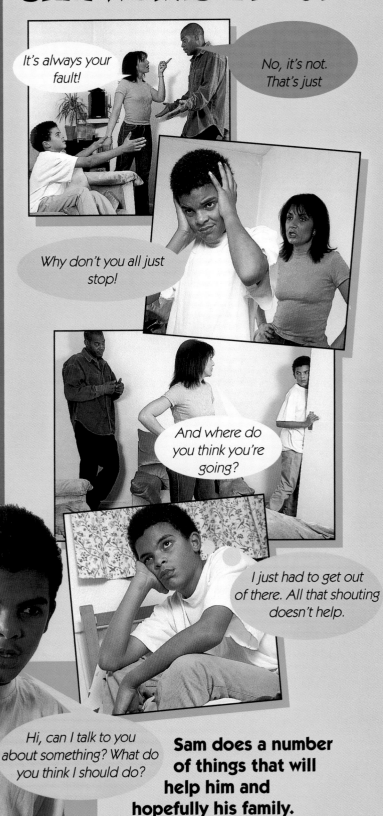

It's always your fault!

No, it's not. That's just

Why don't you all just stop!

And where do you think you're going?

I just had to get out of there. All that shouting doesn't help.

I'm really upset about what's happening. Can we talk about it?

Hi, can I talk to you about something? What do you think I should do?

Sam does a number of things that will help him and hopefully his family. Can you spot them?

SAFETY FIRST STARTS AT HOME

It's never too early to become really aware and responsible for your environment. And one of the best places to start – you guessed it – is at home.

This is the Hazard Family's kitchen. Spot as many health and safety problems as you can.

Maybe the Hazards know a bit more about safety than you first thought. Find six things that could stop an accident turning into a disaster. One is tricky, so look hard.

What to do if there's a gas leak...

1. Tell an adult.
2. Open doors and windows.
3. Don't touch any electrical switches.
4. Don't use a naked flame like a match or candle.
5. Phone the gas people.

What to do if there's a fire...

1. Get out quickly and safely, then call the emergency number.
2. Before opening an inside door, feel it with the back of your hand. If it's hot don't open that door, find another way out.
3. Shout to warn others in the house.
4. If you're stuck in a room, shout out of a window for help. Put something under the door to stop smoke entering.
5. Once outside, stay out!

What to do if there's a serious accident...

1. Phone or ask a neighbour to call the emergency number.
2. Get in contact with a relative or other trusted adult.

What a life saver!

Write a list of emergency telephone numbers on a piece of card and stick it right beside the phone.

What to do if there's a stranger hanging around your home...

1. Don't go up and say 'hello'. Dur!
2. Go inside quickly and quietly or stay inside.
3. Tell an adult and explain what's worrying you.

21

RESPECTFULLY YOURS...

THE Y.C. EXCLUSIVE INTERVIEW

Young Citizen's intrepid reporter, Tel Meall, tracks down Brooke Murray to find out what she knows (or doesn't know) about respect.

TM: What do you think about respect?

BM: Is it a rock band or something?

TM: Ah, no. Respect is something that comes from inside and helps us to live in harmony with others.

BM: Oh, so just what is this respect thing?

TM: If you have respect for people, you consider their feelings, you're polite to them, treat them fairly and you would do them no harm. You can also respect the environment, different cultures and religions and the ways people choose to live.

BM: Cool! But does that mean being polite to my totally gross brother?

TM: Yes, but when you call him 'gross' you're not exactly considering his feelings, are you?

BM: Yeh, but he's nasty to me.

TM: But if you show him some respect, he'll catch on and then shower you with respect.

BM: Wicked! So how do I know if I respect people and if they – especially my brother – respect me?

TM: Do this quiz to find out.

WHERE'S YOUR RESPECT?

1 Your family has a special get-together today, but a friend asks you to their house. Do you …
a) Say you'd love to but not today?
b) Say yes and ask a parent for a lift?

2 You're with friends and see your great aunt, do you …
a) Go and say hello?
b) Go and hide?

3 A big brother is studying for an exam. Do you …
a) Turn down your music and leave him alone?
b) Call him a swot and do everything you can to bug him?

4 You're a vegetarian. What would your meat-eating brother say?
a) Nothing. You don't knock him about what he eats.
b) He calls you a loony and waves sausages in your face.

5 A friend breaks a treasured family heirloom. What do you do?
a) You and your friend own up to it.
b) You say 'Oh, that old piece of tat' as you hide it in the bottom of the bin.

6 Your best friend is from another country and has different traditions to you. What does your family do?
a) They treat her like they treat everyone – with respect!
b) They don't exactly make her welcome.

HOW DID YOU DO?

All As – You and your family have mega-respect for each other. You consider each other's feelings and respect each other's possessions and privacy. You also respect other lifestyles, cultures and traditions.

Mostly As – OK, but a little work needs to be done. Drop the word 'respect' in your conversation as a way of jogging your family's memory. If they're still in the dark, give them this quiz to do.

All Bs – Sad, too sad. If there's no respect then there's no harmony. It's up to you to take that first respectful step. Go to it!

ALL I ASK FOR IS A LITTLE RESPECT

I WANT SOME TOO!

You looked at showing respect for others on pages 22-3. Now it's time to revel in some self-respect.

SELF-RESPECT HAS NOTHING TO DO WITH ...

... how you look
... what possessions you've got
... having a devoted band of fans
... getting your own way
... being snooty

SELF-RESPECT HAS EVERYTHING TO DO WITH ...

..... truly, madly, deeply liking yourself
..... knowing yourself and being honest even about the bad bits
..... having opinions but tolerating those of others
..... never doing anything to harm yourself or your amazing potential
..... not letting anyone bring you down or harm you

RIGHT-ON SELF-RESPECT

Can you identify with any of these?

"My mum used to say that I wouldn't be popular if I was fat. She's so wrong. People like me for what I am, not what I look like." **Jo**

"My sister is excellent at everything. I don't mind because she's the first to congratulate me when I do something really good." **Marty**

"If I goof up badly it's no good moping about it. I just tell myself to try harder next time." **Ahmed**

"I might walk with a limp, but I've got loads of self-respect. I don't think my friends even notice my funny walk any more." **Emerson**

THE GETTING OF SELF-RESPECT

STARRING BILLY AS THE DOORMAT

FURBALL THE CAT AS HERSELF

A V. WISE FILM PRODUCTION

WHY DO YOU LET THEM CALL YOU THOSE HORRIBLE NAMES?

THEY'VE ALWAYS CALLED ME STUPID AND USELESS, SO WHY FIGHT IT?

YOU'RE NOT USELESS OR STUPID. YOU'VE JUST LET THEM CONVINCE YOU.

WELL, DOESN'T THAT SHOW I'M STUPID?

THIS IS GOING TO BE HARDER THAN I THOUGHT. I'LL HAVE TO REMIND BILLY OF ALL THE NEAT THINGS HE'S DONE.

LATER

OH YEAH, I FORGOT ABOUT THAT.

AND THEN THERE WAS THAT KID YOU STOOD UP FOR...

A LOT LATER

BOY, I'VE DONE SOME GREAT THINGS. THEY SHOULDN'T CALL ME THOSE NAMES.

ZZZ

THE BIG QUESTION

How's your self-respect? Knocking them dead at the top of the charts or limping along at the bottom?

YOU'RE NOT GOING OUT LIKE THAT!

Ever heard the saying: From little acorns grow mighty oaks? Well, lots of family disagreements start out as little spats and because they're not sorted out they snowball into mega-disagreements. This is how it happened between Rachel and her Mum ...

Oh, Mum, you're so sad.

Nag, nag, nag. Do this. Do that.

Go and get changed, and do it now!

And where would you be if I didn't nag you?

I'd be somewhere nice, that's where!

WHAT DO YOU LOOK LIKE! (Scenario 1)

Oh, so you don't like it here. Is that it?

Here we go again.

That's it. You're not going anywhere, ever!

SHARP POINTS TO PONDER

Have Rachel and her Mum sorted anything out? Do you think they'll argue like this again? Why? Spot these things: a command, a disrespectful answer, shouting and faces and gestures that are bound to annoy.

26

EVER HEARD OF COMPROMISING?

If you're always having the same sort of arguments over and over, maybe it's time to find solutions that are okay with everyone. This is called a compromise.

A COMPROMISE WON'T HAPPEN IF THERE'S ...

shouting
dig-the-heels-in
   stubborness
no respect for each
   other

A COMPROMISE WILL HAPPEN IF THERE'S ...

talking
willingness to be
   flexible
respect

Let's look at how Miles and his Dad found a compromise.

Do you think that's the right thing to wear. It's a special party, isn't it?

Yeh, but everyone wears this sort of stuff.

Maybe it's just the jeans that don't work.

WHAT DO YOU LOOK LIKE! (Scenario 2)

Could be. I'll try on another pair.

I don't look like a nerd or anything, do I?

You, look like a nerd? Never!

Ready to go?

You bet!

Ah, aren't happy endings just the greatest?

Act 1, no scene
Learning to talk and not argue is so crucial that it's worth a bit of practice. Why don't you and a parent act out a scene where you both want to watch different TV programmes at the same time. Don't forget – no shouting, rude faces or cheeky quips, just a happy ending!

I DIDN'T SAY ANYTHING

Imagine this: you're sitting at the dinner table with your family when a parent says something unbelievable. You don't say anything but you still get into trouble. Do you know why? Because your body has done the talking for you. In body language you said to your parent "You're so sad!"

Let's see how good you are at reading body language. Match the body language to the caption.

"I'm seriously miffed"

"You're boring me!"

"I don't care, what you say"

Imagine someone in your family is sending these silent messages to you. How would you feel?
a) pretty angry
b) pleased that your family shows their feelings
c) upset that they're treating you with no respect.

The thing about body language is that it works both ways. Imagine the itzy-bitzy arguments that wouldn't flare into big ones if everyone used "I'm friendly" body language.

HOW TO STOP AN ARGUMENT WITH A SMILE

"I'm here to work this out. I don't want to argue."

"I'm listening real hard."

"I'm friendly."

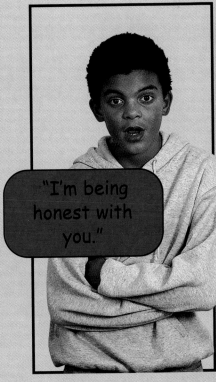

"I'm being honest with you."

Try these at home:

1. All change! Swap roles for a day with kids becoming the adults and vice versa. When you put yourself in someone else's position (and in their shoes) it's easier to understand their point of view.

2. Words count: Try listening to yourself and your family. How many times do you say a really warm "Hello" to each other, ask how someone's feeling or say something nice to them? Chances are it's not often enough. Get the ball rolling by putting down this book and getting on with the friendly chit-chat!

Shh!
Have you heard an argument in a cinema? No? Want to know why? Because when people are sitting really close they talk in whispers and it's almost impossible for an argument to start. Shouting, on the other hand, drives people apart and not just to opposite corners of a room. Once there's all this distance between you, the shouting continues. So to bring you and your family together and to put a silencer on an argument, talk in hushed tones and snuggle up.

29

Glossary

Compromise When disputes are settled in a way that is agreed by everyone, with each person giving up a little of what they want. This is often a good solution as everybody has respected the viewpoints of others.

Culture A whole way of life for a group of people. Other people's cultures can seem alien to us, but learning about them can help us understand other people and their way of life.

Environment Our surroundings. They can exist on any scale for example, your home and school are both environments. The tank your goldfish lives in is its environment. On a bigger scale our planet is our environment.

Faith Having trust or confidence in somebody or something. If you are faithful you do not break promises or try to do something behind someone else's back. If you have faith in a religion it means following its rules and beliefs.

Harmony A musical harmony is a combination of notes and chords that work well together. When people are in harmony, they live and work together without clashing.

Loyalty This means not letting someone down, but sticking by them. Loyalty is really tested when there are troubles or disagreements between people. Sometimes people's loyalties can be split many ways.

Respect Listening to others and learning to understand their way of life and their beliefs. It is also about being polite to others.

Self-respect Believing in yourself and your ideas and treating yourself well.

Tolerance Letting others follow different beliefs and ways of living and respecting that their beliefs may be different from yours.

Books to read

Life Strategies for Teens
by Jay McGraw (Simon & Schuster, 2001)

My Crazy Life: How I Survived My Family
edited by Allen Flaming & Kate Scowen (Annick Press, 2003)

Wise Guides: Family Break-up
by Matt Whyman (Hodder Wayland, 2005)

Useful contacts

Safety brochures about fire and home safety can be obtained through your local council's health and safety officer, the Royal Society for the Prevention of Accidents (RoSPA) on 0121 248 2000, and electricity and gas suppliers' education services. Your library may also have a good selection of information leaflets.

For brochures about keeping safe at school, when out and at home, contact Kidscape at 2 Grosvenor Gardens, London SW1W 0DH or call 020 7730 3300.

Picture acknowledgments:
All pictures are from the Wayland Picture Library with the exception of the following agency pictures: Tony Stone 5 (top left), Angela Hampton 5 (top right), 7 (middle right), Bubbles 13 (bottom right), 15 (bottom right), 18 (top right), 23.

Author acknowledgements
With thanks to RoSPA, Hampshire Fire and Safety and Transco for their advice on the text.

Index